D0095913

The Art of the First Date

The Art of the First Date

Because Dating's Not a Science—It's an Art

Hayley DiMarco
and Michael DiMarco

Revell
Grand Rapids, Michigan

© 2006 by Hungry Planet

Published by Fleming H. Revell
a division of Baker Publishing Group
P.O. Box 6287, Grand Rapids, MI 49516-6287
www.revellbooks.com

Printed in the United States of America

All rights reserved. No part of this publication may be repro-
duced, stored in a retrieval system, or transmitted in any form
or by any means—for example, electronic, photocopy, record-
ing—without the prior written permission of the publisher. The
only exception is brief quotations in printed reviews.

      Library of Congress Cataloging-in-Publication Data
DiMarco, Hayley.
    The art of the first date / Hayley DiMarco and
  Michael DiMarco.
       p.   cm.
    ISBN 10: 0-8007-3148-4 (pbk.)
    ISBN 978-0-8007-3148-9 (pbk.)
    1. Dating (Social customs) 2. Man-woman relation-
ships. I. DiMarco, Michael. II. Title.
HQ801.D563 2006
646.7'7—dc22   2006003744

Published in association with Yates & Yates, LLP, Literary Agents,
Orange, California.

THE
MARRIABLE
GALLERY

of Modern
Dating
Art

"First Date" Wing
-main floor-

5
The Art of Flirting
(page 53)

4
The Art of
Communication
(page 45)

6
Unveiling Your Masterpiece:
a.k.a. The Big Day
(page 81)

8
The Art of Saying
Goodnight
(page 113)

7
The ~~Art~~ Curse of the
Nice Guy
(page 107)

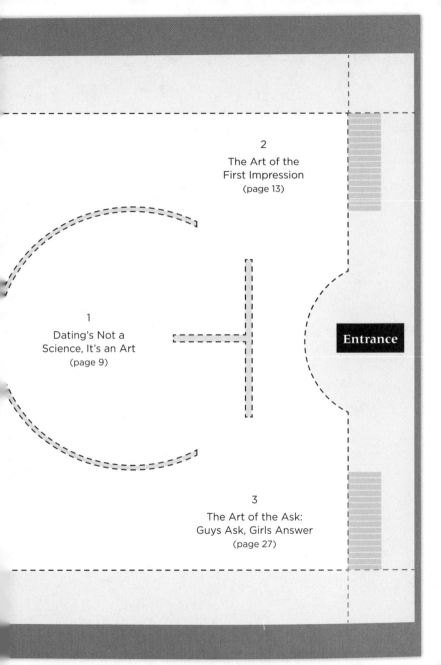

2
The Art of the
First Impression
(page 13)

1
Dating's Not a
Science, It's an Art
(page 9)

3
The Art of the Ask:
Guys Ask, Girls Answer
(page 27)

Entrance

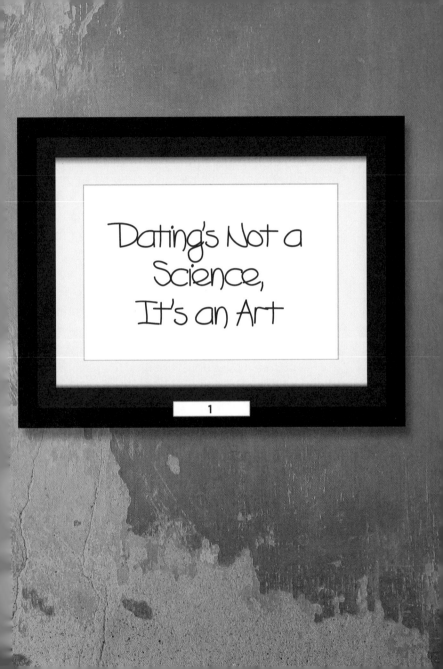

Dating's Not a
Science,
It's an Art

1

In the 21st century, hardly any technological innovation surprises us anymore. Ten thousand songs on one iPod? Sure. Hundreds of movies too? Not a stretch. A voice chip that can be implanted into your cat to make it recite the Declaration of Independence? Um . . . okay, maybe that's a stretch. But you get the picture.

So it shouldn't surprise us to hear of technological advances in "finding a soul mate." Personality profiles, psychological studies, and genetic mapping are all interesting tools for looking inward for insights on ourselves. And some would have us believe they're a foolproof way of finding Mr. or Ms. Right. But do we ever stop to think that a 52 percent divorce rate didn't exist back when people traded livestock for a mate?

Personality profiling aside, even the way we think and emote as men and women has been blurred by a scientific approach to life. Many would encourage us to think that men and women are really the same 'cept for the plumbing. That if you take a man with particular interests, values, goals, and temperament and add a woman with the same interests, values, goals, and temperament—voila!—instant compatibility and good communication automatically result.

When it comes down to it, though, it's not that simple. Communication and relationships between the sexes isn't science. It's an art. Unfortunately, how single men and women should act around each other—as *men* and as **women**—has become a lost art.

Instead of experts teaching men how to woo a woman and exude confidence and protection, counselors are telling men to become more like women. Be more emotionally vulnerable, share your fears, constantly need the relationship defined. Cry.

Crying *is not* the best way to win women over.

Meanwhile, women are told they don't need a man. That they're somehow inferior beings if they aren't aggressive and don't go after what they want. That they're not in control unless they pick up the check and open their own door.

11

Yes, dating is becoming a lost art amid society's attempts to make us all equal (read: the same) and science's best efforts at safeguarding against divorce. In this new series of *Marriable* books, we hope we can help single men and women to fall back in love with the art of dating and to set fire to the lie that men and women are the same. As you read *The Art of the First Date* and digest its practical advice, remember that you're not mixing the perfect scientific formula, you're translating your wishes and intentions in a way that fulfills what the other person is looking for while not scaring them off. And since love can start with just a cup of coffee, let's step back and appreciate *The Art of the First Date.*

The Art
of the First
Impression

2

Impressionism is a style in which the artist captures the image of an object as someone would see it if they just caught a glimpse of it. How another person sees you after only a "glimpse" is called a first impression.

Most people with any social skills would agree, first impressions are very important. From job interviews to appearances in traffic court, how you look, how you carry yourself, and what you say all leave a lasting impression, good or bad. And dating is no different. How your date views you in the first fifteen minutes of the date will set the tone for the rest of the night. Not to mention that their quick take will be a determining factor as to whether you have a chance for a second date.

In actuality, most first impressions start before a guy even asks a girl out. This is true in all asking scenarios except for the Grocery Store Ask (see pages 32–42 for different types of "asks"). Think about it: when a guy finally gets around to asking a girl from work out for a date, she's already watched him spill copier toner all over his pants, heard him gripe about

"According to William Thourlby in 'You Are What You Wear,' we make ten psychological judgments in a first impression including success level, economic status, integrity, education level, social position, level of sophistication, economic heritage, social heritage, educational heritage and moral character."

—Forbes Magazine
(November 1995)

This would fall under the "not so good" category for first impressions, unless your date has a passion for bacon.

overpriced Chicklets-style gum, and smelled him when he came back to work without showering after a noon workout at the gym. Now, does this mean that you have no hope of getting a date with people who **really** know you? Maybe! If anything, it should illustrate the fact that even when you're taking a voluntary break from dating, you're still making first impressions that will influence whether he asks you out and whether she'll say yes once you take the dating ritual off pause.

Guys, before asking a girl out on a first date, ask yourself these two questions: "What is her current impression of me?" and "Will that stop her from saying yes?" Be honest in evaluating yourself. One thing women don't go for is a man who isn't in touch with reality. A guy like that doesn't make her feel safe. So if you've been acting like a total whack job around her and you see her dating (or interested in) more serious guys, you're going to have to change her first impression of you if you really want to get to know her more.

Likewise, ladies, if you want to attract a certain someone to make that leap of faith and ask you out, you're going to have to ask the same questions: "What is his current impression of me?" and "Will that stop him from asking me out?" If you've been "one of the guys" around the office, the guy most likely will never ask you out until you become "chaseable." A chaseable girl is one who knows that guys like a moving target and don't want to date a buddy. Sure, they'll go out with you—that is, until their new girlfriend comes along and you suddenly feel a little less feminine and more like one of the guys. For more on this topic, read the chapter "How Being Just Friends Is a Waste of Time" in our book *Marriable*.

In short, before you ask or get asked, you may have to reframe your first impression to be more desirable to the opposite sex. "But shouldn't I be able to just be me?" you ask. That statement screams, "I think I'm perfect," or "I'm too lazy to change." Think about it. Everyone has room for improvement. We've heard many a lonely single say, "My soul mate will fit me perfectly so neither of us will have to change." HA! More often than not, "soul mates" expose our weaknesses so that we actually become stronger people and partners through the relationship.

17

For now, though, let's get back to the first date. Let's assume that the asking is done and the date is today. Isn't this exciting?

So what makes for a good first impression on a first date? Here are a few of the basics:

- **Dress for the occasion**—Don't show up to meet for coffee wearing a suit or cocktail dress, just like you shouldn't wear shorts and a polo for an evening on the town.

- **Make eye contact**—Avoid the "stalker stare," but practice making eye contact both when you're talking and when your date is talking.

- **Take turns talking**—Nothing turns a quality date off more than a one-sided conversation. There's got to be give-and-take.

- **Be sincerely interested in listening to the other person**—Active listening involves head nodding, parroting back key words and phrases, and the stereotypical psychotherapist "hmms" and "ahhs." But sometimes we use those tools to cover our disinterest. Just think about the last phone call you got from a relative who never lets you get a word in edgewise

Hayley

When Michael and I first met for coffee I was impressed by the fact that he was already there and had gotten a table for us and everything. He made a great first impression by being so prepared, making great eye contact, but not too much, and by being such a good talker. After about 15 minutes of being with him I felt comfortable enough to hint at being hungry so we could continue the date over dinner.

Michael

Yeah, I was in town on business and I literally scouted out the coffee shop Hayley wanted to meet at and made sure I knew where it was hours before we would be meeting so I knew I wouldn't be late and could be there before her. Being late for a first date or getting lost isn't a good first impression.

The Art of the First Impression

or repeats the same story over and over. If you get busted for "fake listening," the relationship is probably already over.

Remember the other person's name—You probably think this last one is stupid, but seriously, we've actually heard of people forgetting. This guy kept calling his date the wrong name the whole night, even after she corrected him. Needless to say, not a very good first impression, and one he couldn't overcome for a second date!

Green Flags That Lead to a Good First Impression:

genuine

sense of humor

creativity

confidence

achievement

fitness

contentment

good posture

good conversationalist

humility

strength

playful

driven

makes eye contact

The Art of the First Impression

**Red Flags That
Lead to a Bad First
Impression:**

self-centered
polarizing
overly materialistic
doesn't make eye
contact
poor conversationalist
highly cynical
dislikes learning
immature
indecisive
ignores unimportant
people
relives old dating
stories
whines and complains
only interested in sex
manipulator

Sometimes a bad first impression is just in the cards. You tried to do everything right, but you couldn't stop talking (or couldn't start). Or maybe you ventured into the TMI zone, sharing how you want to be married and having babies within 18 months. Happens all the time. Here's what you can try to get the other person to give you a second shot.

- **Plead temporary insanity**—Try flattering the other person while poking fun at yourself with something like, "Do you have this effect on all your dates—that they get so nervous they overshare?" No guarantees on this one, but if you knock off this particular behavior, they might just chalk it up to nerves.
- **Blame it on substance abuse**—Okay, not mood enhancers or illegal drugs, but maybe a tad too much caffeine or your new allergy medication ("Gotta get that prescription switched to a nonhallucinogenic!").
- **Disavow ownership**—Say something like, "Okay, now that I've said everything my mother wanted me to say . . ."

23

The IOU response—This "let me make it up to you" shouldn't sound too desperate. A comment like "I soooo owe you another outing sans the chatter" or "How about on the next date you go out with my smooth, charming twin brother, and he'll lock Mr. Awkward in the basement?"

Framing the Chapter

When it comes to creating a good first impression, remember that much of what you're communicating to the other person is nonverbal. After that, the next to shine (or rust) is your personality, which includes your words and actions. A winning attitude is one that is warm, enthusiastic, and truly interested in others. People tend to spend a lot of time alone when they act bored, angry, or bitter.

Remember, good first impressions get you into the game but don't guarantee much past the first or second date. Much like a watercolor painting, first impressions give a glimpse of who you are or how you want to be viewed—until the fire hose of reality hits your canvas. At that point, you'll be exposed as either a fraud or a true work of art in progress.

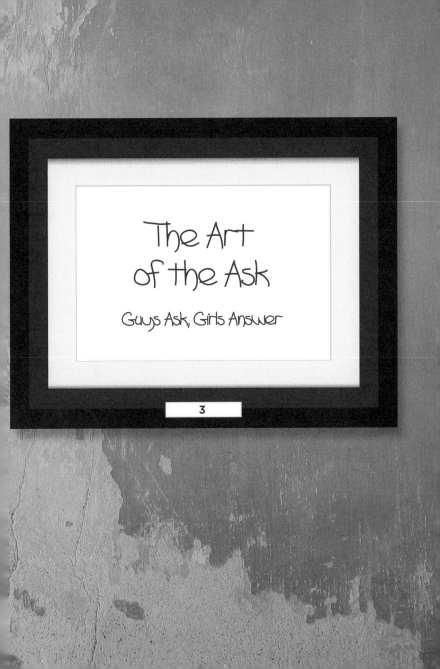

The Art of the Ask

Guys Ask, Girls Answer

3

A starving artist may be passionate about his art, but he will take his involuntary weight loss to the extreme if he never approaches gallery owners to display his work. But art galleries don't have to be his only option. Art is displayed and even sold at restaurants, cafés, and other places of business. An artist who keeps his eyes and options open for displaying his talents typically has more success in getting seen.

In this way, the dating world parallels the art world. A typical single might bemoan the fact that there are "no quality ones left" and throw their hands up in the air. But a confident and *Marriable* male will learn the various and ever-expanding venues in which to approach a woman for a date and will recognize the benefits and drawbacks of that particular "ask" going in. And the *Marriable* woman will be ready to notice the courageous act of the ask in the strangest of circumstances. So before we venture out on our first date, let's examine the Art of the Ask.

There are only two hard and fast rules about asking someone out on a first date:

1. **The guy always asks.**

2. **There are never any exceptions to rule #1.**

We know, we know, a lot of the sensitive guys and confident girls out there are incensed at our backward thinking. But instead of going into a detailed explanation of why we're right and the sensi-guys and confi-girls are wrong, we're just going to say, "Why haven't you read *Marriable* yet?"

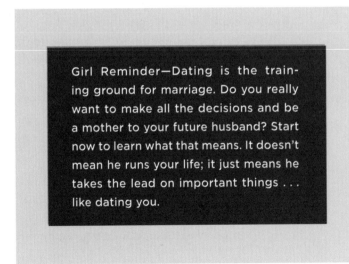

Girl Reminder—Dating is the training ground for marriage. Do you really want to make all the decisions and be a mother to your future husband? Start now to learn what that means. It doesn't mean he runs your life; it just means he takes the lead on important things . . . like dating you.

How to Ask a Girl Out

This section is for guys, because ladies, if you are asking a guy out, you are just asking for heartache. Guys are wired to be the instigators, the aggressors. Throughout time guys have been the ones who kill the animals, go to war, and save the land. They are the ones who love a challenge so much that they shape their whole lives around it. Like it or not, they were made to be the ones to ask, not you. Sure it's the 21st century, sure you *can* ask, sure it's hip to ask, but in the end it's a silly decision that is only based on your pride and your fear that the right guy will never come at the right time to ask you just the right way.

So guys, read on, this advice is for you! And girls, you can read on too to see if a guy is date-worthy.

No history? Start small—If you barely know the woman, start with coffee or lunch. If you've got a working relationship and have done lunch or coffee on a platonic or professional level, move to the p.m. so she knows it's clearly a date.

Ask her out for a specific event—Don't say, "Hey, we should go out sometime" or "You wanna do something?" Come on now, be a man, stand up and ask for what you want. "Would you like to go out to dinner next Friday night? Say 7:00?" or "Hey, I've got two tickets to Monster Trucks of Death, would you like to go next Saturday?"

Don't ask her when a bunch of people are around—This is more for your protection than hers. If she says no, you can save yourself a lot of embarrassment by not asking her in front of other friends or co-workers.

If she says no, don't ask why—Just say, "Okay, maybe another time," and walk away. If she wants to go out with you, she will give you another date that works, or she may just start flirting with you more.

Never ask her more than twice—If she says no two times in a row, then she probably means no forever, unless she also tells you that she would "love to but she can't this weekend, how about next weekend?" You don't want to be a pest, but you also need to make sure she just isn't really busy.

Ask her yourself—Don't ask your friend to find out if she will date you. Ask for yourself; don't be a middle schooler and find out if it's safe or not. Be a man!

Ask her out for one date at a time—Don't get all greedy and ask her out for several dates at once. Girls like a bit of mystery. When you are all over her too soon, it's a real turnoff.

Be direct—Say "Would you like to _____?" Avoid things like, "I know you are busy but maybe one day I was wondering if you . . ." Get to the point and get to it fast. Don't be a wimp. Be direct and know what you want.

Now let's talk about the different types of asks, remembering that an ask can be for a date or just for contact information like an email address or phone number.

The Grocery Store Ask

How many times have you heard "a great place to meet singles is in the produce or frozen food section"? Because this ask is most often an impulse/*carpe diem*/gut feeling type of ask, we'll explain it a bit.

While there's no compatibility or spirituality litmus test in observing someone handle baked goods, the Grocery Store Ask shows a distinct level of confidence from a guy who strikes up a conversation cold with an unknown

"You know, it's dangerous for you to be here in the frozen food section . . . because you could melt all this stuff."

—Steve Martin as Vinny in the movie *My Blue Heaven*

The Art of the Ask

female. The chances of seeing someone attractive to you in public and having key interests, faith, and goals in common are extremely slim, akin to the chance of buying a winning lottery ticket. But that's where this ask's charm lies as well. It's a great "throw yourself off the dock" way of getting over your fear of rejection . . . because your odds of being rejected are high. (For more on handling rejection or dishing it out in healthy ways, read our book *The Art of Rejection*.) This ask has a tad more potential in venues like a coffee shop or gym you frequent, places where you've been able to make eye contact, strike up a conversation, and flirt a tad as a foundation.

The one thing vital to the Grocery Store Ask is a good intro, usually involving humor. Look, we're not going to give you a bunch of surefire pickup lines because there aren't any. And besides, if we did, everyone would be using the same ones.

Hayley

C'mon, at least give them one for each type of ask!

Michael

Who am I, Fonzie? Wait, don't answer that. . . . Okay, here's what I would say to you if I saw you at the store with a bag of cat food: "You know, Meow Mix is really good on top of ice cream. Gotta love the sprinkles."

Hayley

Oh, Cheesemeister, you had me at "meow"!

Remember, ladies, if the guy gets up the nerve to try an ask in the grocery store, at least be polite in rejecting him. If you're at all curious, don't give him your number but offer an anonymous email address instead. Safety first! Then you can see if his background and interests match up well with his courage.

The Art of the Ask

An old saying goes, "Never dip your pen in the company ink." Of course, now pens contain their own ink, and we're pretty sure most companies don't have a BYOP policy. But if we're not mistaken, this adage basically meant don't date people from work. Perhaps an updated version would be "Don't swap personal files on the company server." But we digress.

Company ink

There are dangers in dating someone from your daily routine, and doubly so when it comes to your employment situation. Sometimes breaking up with a co-worker can throw such a wrench in things at work that one of you might start looking for a new job. But since hope springs eternal and assuming you've considered all this, let's get your ask on!

With a Co-worker Ask, many times you can set up a date before the date. Coffee or lunch with your co-worker crush is the safest progression to an all-out evening out. Just make sure that it's low-key and happens in the course of a workday. In other words, no making a special trip in on your day off.

The Church Ask is loaded with many of the same pitfalls involved with dating in the workplace. The main difference between the Co-worker Ask and the Church Ask is an avenue of intimacy that isn't present at work or school: spiritual intimacy.

We've heard story after story of singles in church settings having crushes on others at their church but nothing happening except for awkward conversations in group settings or praying together on leadership teams.

Let us just get out in the open that most guys are wary of asking someone out at church for fear of being seen as a shark. There's also a stigma floating around that dating is somehow unbiblical. Just as a reminder to our amateur theologians out there, dating and courtship examples in the Bible were always talked about in the context of social custom and ritual—like multiple wives, marrying your brother's wife if your brother dies, and trading oxen for a wife. Ah, nothing says soul mate like the sweet musk of oxen!

Women in a church setting oftentimes feel the harlot (to use the biblical word) to the guy's shark if they say yes to any Matthew, Mark, or Luke that asks them out. Women

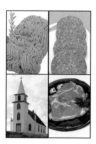

One of these things is not like the others.

feel flirting and dating within the church is some sort of taboo, all the while bemoaning the fact there aren't any great guys to date who share their faith. Talk about a mixed message! Good, godly guys and girls need to accept the fact that there is no better place to meet the opposite sex and have essentials in common than church. Get over the meat market analogy!

Guys need to get over the nice guy curse and become a great guy (see "The ~~Art~~ Curse of the Nice Guy," page 107), while women need to stop fearing a one-on-one date with someone at church will plaster them with a scarlet letter.

The Party Ask

A distant cousin of the Grocery Store Ask, the Party Ask allows for more recon, flirting, and conversation before a guy determines to make the ask. The odds of the woman saying yes also increase dramatically. The key to the Party Ask is access. The guy must look for an opening to strike up a conversation. It's best if he waits until some nonverbal flirting has been

The Art of the Ask

established, unless a formal introduction has been made by a third party.

One thing to remember about the Party Ask is that all the guy needs is a way to contact the female of interest at a later date. Do you know where she works? Does she blog? The party doesn't necessarily need to be the place and time where you ask her out. But if you seem to be spending the entire time together talking, laughing, and flirting, be a man and make your move. A good move is to leave the party before she does (you've got an early morning coming) but say you'd like to continue the conversation and ask if she would like to meet for coffee later in the week.

Unless you were hallucinating, bingo, you're in! Even though you left the party earlier than you planned, you left her wanting more and showed manly self-control. Reward yourself by going home to revel in your victory and watch some late-night TV. You've earned it!

The Online Ask

Some unique circumstances come up in moving from online dating to IRL (In Real Life) dating. If you read ***Marriable***, you know the story of how we met online. If you're looking for love online, or thinking about it, there's one nugget of wisdom we want you to hold tight to your pounding little chest: ***Until you date in real life, you're not dating!*** Get that? You may be emailing, chatting, IMing, and flirting madly throughout, but you're ***not*** dating.

Do you know why? Because it's not real until you meet in real life. Hence the phrase "in real life." Too many times people get ramped up over online conversations and posted profiles, which can potentially be all lies or exaggerations. Not to mention it's possible to have a total lack of physical chemistry once you see the person.

We know, we know, we're so shallow! Let's get real: unless you're going to conduct your entire dating and marriage relationship online and never see each other, you need to consider how your potential mate fills your space. That's not just physical appearance but mannerisms, nonverbal communication, how they treat you and others when you're out together—basically, things you can't find out until you date in real life!

Now that some of you have judged us as bitter or pessimistic, may we remind you that meeting online worked fabulously well for us! In fact, we highly recommend it. We just don't want you to fall into a make-believe world that doesn't truly exist until you replicate it IRL.

Note to the girls (but important for the guys to figure out as well): how does one make the move from online to IRL? Slowly and safely. Just like IRL, a woman should wait for the man to suggest a date and should only accept after she knows enough to feel safe. Do you know his last name? Do you know where he works and what he does for a living? Have you Googled him? Try seeing if his name is in his company's online staff directory (and his picture matches his profile). If you can't give your best friend enough information to send the FBI after him at his apartment, work, and parents' house, it's too soon for IRL.

Don't ignore the signs. Slowly and safely is the way to go.

And guess what? Women shouldn't be expected to share the same info with the guy. Sure you should tell him what you do for a living, but not to the point of him narrowing down where you work. He definitely shouldn't have your home address, and hopefully you only supplied an anonymous email address (Hotmail, Yahoo, etc.) instead of your work email. Any guy who starts crying, "But that's not fair!" doesn't understand women and their need for security, is scared for his security (not very guy-like), or has something creepy in mind. 'Nuff said.

The progression of the Online Ask is simply this:

1. Email
2. Instant message or online chat
3. Phone (guys, offer your number to the woman so she doesn't have to give out hers, and women, try dialing *67 before you dial the number to block your caller ID)
4. Coffee in a public place (you should each tell a friend all about it and give them links to your date's profile, and you should each have your own transportation)

Meeting online can be a great way to sift through a ton of date possibilities. Just keep the medium in mind and guard your heart and safety in the process.

Speaking of meeting online,
come visit us at www.marriable.com.

Framing the Chapter

Guys who don't ask and women who don't expect them to do so set themselves up for an awkward dance set to absolutely no music. The ask is the guy's opportunity to show leadership, initiative, and, gulp, interest! Likewise, women need to back off and stop enabling men to be lazy wimps. When women do the asking, it sets the tone for the entire relationship. It says, "If anything's gonna get done around here, I'm doing it instead of waiting on the guy."

Gentlemen, it's time to stop being so gentle. The worst a woman can say is no. Men need to get the art of the ask drilled into their heads (and hearts) and to recognize that it's necessary for them to take the role of the gambler instead of the role of the wimp. It's time for men to take a chance and show interest. You can do it!

The Art of
Communication

4

One of the major keys to a successful first date is the nebulous topic of ***communication***. Whether your communication style leans toward oversharing or that of a shrinking violet, how you communicate on your first date is a major contributor to your success getting a second. Let us explain the ways first-daters can trip over their tongues.

The ~~Art~~ Curse of Oversharing

Most artists we know agree that a work of art should speak for itself. Have you ever known someone who so overexplained their school project, work effort, or artistic creation that the work actually lost much of its luster because of the creator's blathering? Resisting the urge to overshare is one of the hardest habits for the extroverted "people person" to overcome. But curbing your enthusiasm a tad will allow some mystery to remain. And when there's mystery, there's usually a second date.

Michael

In sales they call it "talking someone out of the sale." I once worked with a guy who would have people ready to buy the product we were selling within 5 minutes of seeing it, but after 15 minutes of him talking, the potential customer was walking away empty-handed.

Hayley

I've known a lot of women who do the same thing with men. As females we're taught that sharing means intimacy, so it makes sense to share as much as possible to bond with the other person. More often than not, women don't understand that they're losing their emotional virginity on the first date!

Michael

And meanwhile, the guy feels like an avalanche of pressure just dumped on him, and he's frantically digging himself out thinking, "I knew I should've stayed home and watched *CSI*." But I know I was guilty of doing the same thing back in my "nice guy" days.

Hayley

Riiiight. When the guy shares so much so soon that the woman starts feeling like the man, she starts putting up this invisible wall, trying to distance herself from the overly emotional male across from her. Been there, done that. Not pretty.

47

So what are some helpful hints to keep you from over-sharing, you ask? Ask yourself these questions:

> **Are you about to share something that you wouldn't tell a stranger on a bus?**
>
> **Does it have to do with an old flame?**
>
> **Is your mouth starting to utter the words "marriage" or "kids"?**
>
> **Is your date finishing their main course while you're not even done with your salad?**

If you find yourself guilty of one of the above, fear not, there is hope. The one surefire method to keep from over-sharing: ask the other person questions. When you're the one asking questions, the pressure is off you to fill the conversational airwaves. In fact, you come off as genuinely interested in the other person. Now, typically you're going to get asked the same questions in return, but you can listen to your date's responses and answer in turn with appropriate responses. Basically, you're listening and crafting a response not quite as complete as your date's.

Plain and simple, the oversharer looks desperate.

Major Female Fumble from *Marriable*

Women mess up when they talk too much. We've never once heard a man say, "I just wish she'd talk more." Generally that's a female complaint. But have you ever thought that maybe he doesn't talk enough because you don't let him get a word in edgewise, ladies? Relationships are give-and-take. If the talking is all one-sided, don't blame it on him. Just maybe you are hogging all the words.

We like to refer to women who talk too much as "giving up their emotional virginity." That is, they give away every ounce of themselves emotionally, and the result is the same as giving themselves up sexually—they are exposed and vulnerable to so much pain and heartache if and when the relationship ends.

49

The Art of Turn-Taking

Much like the oversharer, the person with an overbearing communication style looks desperate. Desperate for attention. Desperate for control. The main difference between the oversharer and overbearer is that one is sharing way too much personal information, and the other just has diarrhea of the mouth. Equal turn-taking when communicating on a first date (or subsequent dates, for that matter) ensures that you both learn enough about each other and how you express yourselves.

Now, someone can be supernervous on a first date and get a bad case of jabberjaw that's atypical for them. Maybe that's endearing to you, at least endearing enough for a second date so you can see if they regain their footing. But likewise, it could have the opposite reaction and irritate you to the core. Hasta la vista, baby.

On the other hand, one of the most frustrating things in the world is going out on a date with a shrinking violet or shy guy. You almost feel like you have to hold up both sides of the conversation.

Michael

There was a period in my dating career when I found myself getting into relationships with a lot of violets. I finally realized I was holding up both ends of the conversation early in the dating process and had convinced myself that things were going to turn out great! Can you say Narcissus?

Hayley

I could see a little "overbearing" in your past. Ha! So how did you fix that bad habit?

Michael

The turning point was when I was on a first date and the same old thing was happening: me talkie, she laughie. We made plans for a second date, and driving home I thought, "Did she do anything but laugh tonight?" So on the second date, I made a little small talk to get things going and then waited for her to contribute. Nothing. Nada. Zip. More pregnant pauses than a maternity ward. I just smiled and ate dinner. Inexplicably, at the end of the date she said, "I had a really great time!" Nice girl with very low miles on her voice box.

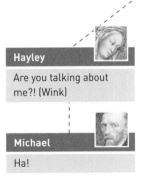

Hayley

Are you talking about me?! (Wink)

Michael

Ha!

If you're a shrinking violet or shy guy, let us encourage you to find some courage! Look, you aren't abandoning the "true you" by coming out of your shell a little. Most SVs and SGs tell us, "It's just when I first meet someone that I'm that way." Do we have to keep you after class to reread the chapter on first impressions?

Look, we know it's nerve-wracking putting yourself out there, risking rejection. But it's that way for everyone. It's just that some have come to understand the Art of Rejection better than others. (*The Art of Rejection* is available at better bookstores everywhere!) The sooner you start walking a little taller, looking people in the eye, and treating dates like a friendly interview process, the sooner you'll realize that you have more control over your love life than you know.

The Art
of Flirting

5

Okay, this could be a book in and of itself (maybe it will be!), but for now, let's just cover the basics. In "First Impressions" (page 13) we already covered how important nonverbal communication is. You may have even used some of the flirting recommendations in *Marriable* to get you on a first date. Now let us give you some pointers on how your nonverbal actions and comments can paint a masterpiece of anticipation using the Art of Flirting.

Flirting sometimes gets a bad rap. And if used improperly it can be a manipulative tool in the hands of a crazed male or female. But if used properly it is a sweet way of telling someone that you think they are special. It's really an art form that allows people to communicate affection and acceptance in playful and fun ways. Most people love to be flirted with; it means that someone thinks they are interesting, funny, or just plain good-looking. It builds up people's self-esteem and gives them energy. Flirting is the best way for two people to know if they like each other in the same way. It's a clue that tells you if you should approach for more or just walk away. Not returning the flirting is a good way to tell someone kindly that you aren't interested. And of course returning the flirting is a good way to show interest in someone without pressuring them to get to moving and ask you out. It makes women more attractive and men more appreciated.

But flirting can be tough if you don't know what you are doing. In fact, it can be downright dangerous in the hands of an amateur. So in the following pages we're going to shed a little light on the subject of flirting. Please note that the flirting we are proposing here is flirting with intent. Never flirt with someone you don't want to date. A person who does that is called a tease. They use flirting to make themselves feel better, and they give flirting a bad rep. Flirting is simply playful banter and nonverbal communication between two people who like one another enough to pursue a relationship. When you flirt with someone you would never consider dating, you are being cruel and unkind.

Also note that flirting, as defined in the pages that follow, isn't used for sexual advances or innuendo. It is simply a gentle and sweet signal to another that you are interested in them and that a next step is appropriate.

Think of a world where flirting is prohibited. For guys it would be a nightmare. They would have no idea who liked them, who would accept a date, and who would leave them to burn. It's a scary proposition, asking a girl out, and without clear evidence that she wants him to ask her, he runs the risk of being shot down or of being inappropriate. Think of a girl who is asked out by a guy she would never be caught dead with. She has no attraction to him and no desire to go out with him, but he's asked, and now she is left with the difficult challenge of telling him no without hurting him or, harder yet, telling him no so he gets it. Some guys can be so doggone aggressive that they won't leave you alone, and then the agony starts.

Even in a world *with* flirting, some guys just don't have a clue.

In a world without flirting, guys are left without a clue. Ask any guy and he'll say he has no idea what women are thinking or what they want, so imagine there's no flirting process and see how much more difficult it all gets. Flirting is an essential step in the dating and mating process. Throwing it out because some people abuse it is throwing the proverbial baby out with the bathwater—and you can go to jail for throwing babies!

56

Like I said, flirting takes skill. It also takes love and kindness. Never use flirting in the following situations:

- when you have a boyfriend/girlfriend already
- when you don't like the guy/girl you are flirting with
- when it's all you do—be picky; don't flirt with everyone or everyone will be confused
- when you are just being cruel
- when you want someone to do something for you
- when they have a boyfriend/girlfriend
- when it is overly sexual (guys are easily turned on, so keep it clean!)

The Art of Mystery

In our book *Marriable* we talked about this idea of letting the guy chase the girl in the chapter called "Women, Shut Up and Be Mysterious." After women read *Marriable*, we get all kinds of comments like "Okay, so how do I become mysterious?" This is our tried-and-true answer on how to make yourself that mystery girl that guys fall head over

57

heels for. And guys, pay attention. If the girl you want to ask out is practicing these flirting techniques, it's time to ask her out!

He calls more. When it comes to the phone, slow it down. He needs to be the one making the most phone calls. Sure, after you are going out for a while, you can call him. But just watch yourself and make sure you aren't the one making the most effort. It's a chasing thing. In order for him to feel like he's chasing you, he needs to feel like he's making the most phone calls. So if he always calls when you are out, you don't have to return every phone call, because you don't want to be calling him as much as he calls you. Relax—if you guys are on good terms and you don't call back right away, he'll call again. Here's a gauge for phone calls:

The 50 percent rule—for every two calls he makes, you give him one (if you really like him).

If you aren't sure how much you like him, go for one in three return phone calls.

If you're not interested at all, don't keep calling him back, even if you are bored. You will give him the wrong idea. Then when you see him at school, work, or church, say hi first and just chat for a second. Keep the conversation on college, work, or church and then move on. Be sure not to flirt.

He says more. I know you love to talk, and you probably talk more than him, but keep your mouth shut more than him when it comes to affection. Let him be the first to tell you how much he cares. Let him chase you with his words. You can return the favor; just don't do it first or more often.

He gives more. Gifts, flowers, attention, all that stuff means major points for the guy, so we think that it's the same for him getting stuff from women. But it isn't. How odd, I know! Men get more of a rush from doing things for women than they do from getting things from women. So if you are heavy on the giving (cards, gifts, back rubs), you aren't doing yourself any favors. He isn't giving you love points for your gifts. He might think they are nice and all, but you score much more on the Love Richter Scale when you graciously accept the things he does for you and gives to you.

Body language. One of the most attractive personality features besides sense of humor is confidence. And truth is, you might not really feel too confident, but that's okay. There is a way to appear confident even if you don't feel like it. It's all about body language. Who wants to be alone with someone who looks like they don't even like to be alone with themselves? So here's what you do so that you look like you actually like yourself and think you are fun to be with:

Stand straight—Stand with your back straight and your feet no farther than 6 inches apart, with your toes pointed in a little bit.

Look him in the eye—Don't be too shy to look him in the eye. That means you think you are worthy of him and that you think he's worthy of you. You don't have to stare; just look for a couple seconds and then look down. He'll get the picture.

Talk—I know it's hard to talk when your crush is drop-dead gorgeous, but you have to do it. Don't clam up; make small talk. Say hi. Ask him how he's doing. Getting the conversation started is a good thing, and it encourages a guy to talk to you more.

Touch your hair—Women already do this without even knowing it, but it's a sure sign to a guy that she's interested. Toss it from one side to the other. Smooth it down. Play with it a little, and an observant guy will get the hint.

Copycat—Watch his body language and make yours the same. If his hand is on his face, put your hand on your face. It is a subconscious way to say, "I agree with you; I'm on your side." And subconsciously he'll get it.

Touch him a little—If you really think a guy is for you, the final stage is to invade his personal space. It doesn't take much, just a brush of your hand on his arm or a bump up against him with your shoulder. Anything that starts to break down the invisible barrier between you is a good flirting technique.

Catch his eye. The best way to catch anyone's eye is to have something unique about you. That might be a really funky scarf or hat or a bizarre bracelet. Anything the guy can use as a conversation starter is always a good idea. Besides, it builds your quirky factor, and quirky is good.

Compliment him. It's polite and just good manners to compliment people, but it also tells a guy that you are interested. So don't overdo it, but do make sure to tell him that you admire or appreciate something about him. He'll love it.

Be fearless. The best flirt is one who is self-confident and fearless, willing to risk rejection just to see what will happen. So don't worry about how the guy will take it—most will love it, we promise. Flirting with someone is one of the biggest compliments you can give them. And if for some odd reason they are antiflirting, then oh well, nothing ventured, nothing gained. Laugh it off and move on. Besides, it will be a great story to tell your friends. We all need something to laugh at about ourselves; it helps make us human.

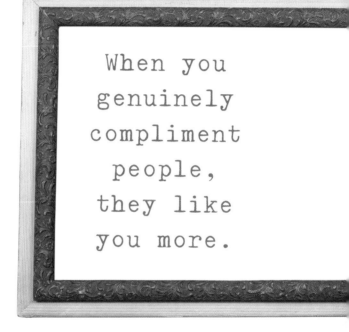

When you
genuinely
compliment
people,
they like
you more.

How to Compliment

Guys and girls want to be complimented in different ways. Don't compliment the way you want to be complimented, because it won't make as much sense to the opposite sex. The basic thing you need to know is that girls like to be complimented on who they are. Their beauty, their brains, their talents, stuff about them as a person. But guys would rather be complimented on what they did than on who they are.

Not making any sense? Check out this chart and maybe you'll start to get it.

Compliments for Guys

That was such a great idea.
I would never have thought of that.
Your shirt is really nice.
I'm having an awesome time.
I had so much fun tonight.
I had a great time talking with you yesterday.
That movie was great.

Compliments for Girls

You are so smart.
I love how creative you are.
You look amazing in that dress.
You're so awesome.
You are so much fun to be with.
You are so great to talk to.
You always pick the best movies.

Does He Really Like You, Like You?

A Quiz

1. It's like you're hiring and he's trying to get the job. It seems like he just loves telling you how great he is and what he's done that's impressive.
   True   False

2. Whenever he sees you, he smiles and looks you right in the eye.   **True   False**

3. On a couple of occasions you have caught him checking out your body—not like a pervert but subtly looking you up and down.   **True   False**

4. He IMs or emails you a lot. He always seems to be online when you are.   **True   False**

5. He calls you just to chat.   **True   False**

6. He asks you a lot of questions about yourself.
   True   False

7. He seems really interested in what you have to say.   **True   False**

8. He makes a lot of nice gestures like offering to buy you coffee or help you with a car problem.
   True   False

Score: Now count up how many "True" answers you have:

True: _____

1–3 True—Not so sure he's into you, girl. Sorry to be the bearer of bad news, but either you have a really shy guy or he just isn't into you like that. Either way, don't try to fix it. Let him be. Let him do what he will. Be strong, and one day a guy will find you to be the dream that you are.

4–5 True—He might just dig you. He's a guy, what do they know about girls? But the signs seem to be pointing in a good direction. He's making some kind of attempt. It might be just for friendship (what a waste of time!), but find out more by returning his flirting, and see where it goes.

6–8 True—He's sold. The guy is gaga for you, in case you were totally clueless. You are making his life wonderful. Keep up the flirting and let him take it where he will, but I'm pretty sure a date is in your future.

The Death of Flirting: What Turns Him Off?

Ladies, here are some surefire flirting dousers that will cool most guys' jets and keep them from asking you out:

Girls who complain all the time—If you want to turn a guy off, then complain about something. Ugh! No one wants to hear how horrible things are, especially guys. A little secret: when you complain about something to a guy, you actually run the risk of making him feel like you are unhappy with him. Guys can take on complaints about something they've given you, thought of, or even done with you as a direct hit. Even if you're complaining about things that don't involve him, news flash: guys are obsessed with fixing things! It's a part of guyness. If you are constantly complaining about things, he gets exhausted trying to fix them or frustrated that he can't. So keep your whining to your mom, your best friend, and your cat.

Girls who don't need a guy—We know it seems weird to the female gender, but believe us when we tell you that guys like to be needed. It's one more part of guyness. If you need no one, you have no purpose in Guyville. That's why guys want to be part of a team, why dads get depressed when they don't have a job, and why guys aren't interested in girls who can do it all themselves. If you don't need him for anything, then you don't need him.

Girls who need him too much—We know, we just said that a guy needs to be needed, but if you need him too much, then that's just as bad as not needing him at all. Part of why you date and wait before you get married is so that you have time to become independent. You have time to become who you are. If you go from needing Daddy to needing a guy like a daddy, you can wear a guy out.

Girls who tell him everything—"Blah, blah, blah." This is what he hears when you talk too much. Don't tell him everything; it's too much for a guy to handle. Best policy? Just tell him good stuff. Make conversation, but keep the intimate, uncomfortable, or way too personal stuff to yourself. We know this seems like such a foreign concept to the feminine psyche since women bond by talking. Jane Doe says, "The more I tell you about me, the more I like you and the more you like me. That's just how it works." But check out two guys hanging out.

Oh, be careful little mouth how much you say.

What do they do together? It gives you a good clue about what they like to do. Do they sit around chatting about their deepest fears? Do they analyze each other's dreams? Do they encourage each other about their fat bottoms and flabby arms? Do they in any way spend their time communicating the way women do? Seems like such a stupid question, we know. But you really need to think about this one. Guys, when they are alone together, avoid deep conversation and go straight for competition, games, sports, and trivia. For the most part guys don't bond by sharing deep emotions. So now why do you think that suddenly, when they are with you, everything they are, think, and feel goes out the window and they become, well, girls? Listen, guys are not girls. Therefore, you can't talk to them like girls. Think about what they like instead of what you like. Novel concept: give others what they want instead of what you want. And give your mouth a break.

SENSITIVE NICE GUY ALERT: The preceding paragraph was for you too!

Girls who always think there is a problem—There's just something about us women that makes us wanna make everyone happy, so when you sense that someone is bummed or upset, your number one goal is to fix it. Trouble is, the way you fix it is by talking about it. And most often, too much. If there is a problem, most of the time a guy will work it out on his own unless he really needs to bring it to your attention. Now, we're not saying don't ever ask if there is a problem. It's just when you think that every little thing is a sign that he is upset, you aren't right; you're just annoying.

Girls who backstab other girls—You think guys aren't watching, but they are. When you go psycho on another girl and do all you can to bring her down, it shows. And it ain't a pretty sight. You might feel good about it, and your girlfriends might applaud you, but to a guy you just look like a witch.

Girls who are jealous—Jealousy isn't a pretty color on anyone (it's not pretty, being green). So if you are jealous, keep it to yourself. Jealousy just means that you don't think that you are as good as the other girl. That makes you look insecure. Try to keep the "mean green" within you under wraps, unless the guy is just totally out of hand

71

in flaunting his "other girls," and in that case, just dump him. Don't use jealousy to change him.

Flirting with Girls: How-tos That Really Work

When you find a woman that you like, one that you would really like to approach for dating, then you need to get the signals going. Asking a girl out cold turkey (a la the Grocery Store Ask, page 32) is kind of a shock to the system. First she needs to see that you are interested and be allowed to show you if she is interested as well. So slow the boat down and try some of these things before you dive in and ask her to do something with you.

Notice her—Women love to be noticed. It makes them feel really special. So make sure she sees you noticing her. Don't act like some kind of construction worker on break, but sneak a peak at her so she catches you.

Look her in the eye—If you can't look a woman in the eyes, you can't get her attention. Girls are all about eyes; they love 'em, and they love it when you look them in the eye.

Be clean, smell good, and check your breath—Smells are really important to women. They get turned on (or off) by what they smell, so do your best to smell good. Take care of your teeth and, yes, keep your breath strips handy.

Your mouthwash just isn't working if your date starts wearing one of these.

Try to get to know her—Women want to be known. They want someone to really know who they are. That means you ask her about herself; you let her talk; you let her express herself. The more she can tell you about herself, the more she'll like you.

Show that you are attracted—Women need clues. They need to know you are interested. Then in turn they will let you know they are attracted. That takes off the edge of fear about asking her out. Explore. Show her you are attracted and see how she reacts. If she is obviously cold, then she's probably not interested.

Smile at her—A smile goes a long way. Everyone loves a smile. So smile at her; it speaks volumes.

73

Be where she is—Find out what she does, what she likes, and show up there. Now, don't become a stalker guy; just explore. If she obviously couldn't care less that you are there, then back off. Don't push yourself on her. But if she shows signs of liking you, you can continue to be where she is.

Give her compliments—Compliments go a long way. A lot of women don't know how to take a compliment, but that doesn't mean you stop. Compliment straight up. Don't make up stuff; really mean it.

Say something funny—Most girls say humor is the most important thing in a guy. That means don't take yourself too seriously. Even if you aren't superfunny, lighten up. Laugh. Enjoy life and she'll love it.

Stand tall—Don't stand all hunched over. She likes a man who stands up straight. It shows your confidence. Stand with your feet 6 to 10 inches apart, and point your toes out just a little.

Make slight contact—Touch her lightly on the back, shoulders, or arm when you help her put her coat on, get the door for her, or guide her across the street.

Be a copycat—People who agree copy each other's body language. If she is leaning forward, then lean forward; if she has her hands on her face, put your hands on your face. Subconsciously she will think you both agree, and that is good.

If she's making this gesture, take the hint and move on.

How Do You Know She Likes You?

- She looks at you and looks away
- She smiles at you
- She giggles
- She touches or flips her hair
- She bites her lip
- She is always where you are
- She compliments you
- She touches your arm or leg lightly
- If none of these are happening, then move on—she probably isn't interested

The Art of Flirting

What a Woman Wants

- To be thought of as beautiful, inside and out
- To be special to someone besides her parents and girlfriends
- To be taken care of
- Small thoughtful gestures
- To be treated like a princess
- To make other girls jealous—i.e., to have a better boyfriend than other girls, a guy who is supersweet, caring, giving, etc.
- To be heard—i.e., someone to listen to her while looking her in the eyes
- To be understood—which means just listening, not trying to fix her
- To find a guy who's less emotional than she is
- To feel safe and protected in the midst of danger
- To be with a guy who doesn't act like a girl

The Death of Flirting: What Turns Her Off?

Guys who act like girls. Don't be overly sensitive. Don't act like your life rides on whether she likes you or not. Take it all like a man, and you will be tons more attractive. She should be the more emotional one. Don't get all girly on her; let her be the female in the relationship.

Guys who are all hands. Women like to know that you think they are hot, but when you are all hands, it's a total turnoff. It says to a girl that all you think is hot is her body, and she wants you to think her mind is hot and her heart is hot and her spirit is hot. So lay off with all the hands all over her.

Guys who never ask. Guys who are too afraid to ask her out and never even make a move will turn her off slowly but surely. Mainly it's because she assumes either there is something wrong with her or you're not man enough to take the risk. So step up to the plate and ask!

Guys who won't take no for an answer. Okay, it's cool for a guy to be the aggressor, the one who goes after the girl, but learn one thing: no means no when it comes to sex and dating. Now, no might be yes when you ask her if anything is wrong and she says no. But if you ask her out and she says no and gives you no other option, she means it. So learn to take no for an answer.

Guys who are self-absorbed. Women love to be the center of your attention. They want to be your favorite person, so when you act like **you** are your fave person, she's out. If you want to date yourself, then by all means be into you, but if you want some lovin' from a woman, lay off with the ego trip.

Guys who fall too fast (i.e., guys who are too nice). A lot of guys peg themselves as nice guys when they get rejected. But a lot of the time it has nothing to do with how nice you are; it's just how fast you are going emotionally. Don't go deeper emotionally than the girl. She likes the excitement of not knowing everything you are thinking and feeling. Keep pace with her, and when you think she is at a new emotional level, you can go there too. Guys, you lead the relationship, and that means it's cool for you to express your love and affection before her, but watch her and don't do anything until you are sure she will accept what you have to say.

Guys who make her be the guy. Inside of every girl is a girly girl, even if she won't admit it. Don't make her be the guy. Carry the stuff, make the plans, pay for things. Take your role so that she can take hers and find out how great it really is to be a girl.

Guys who are wimps. Protect her. Stand up for her. Be a man—not a caveman but a gentleman. Don't be afraid of her, and don't be a wimp around her. Be the man you were made to be, and she'll love you for it.

Got surefire flirting tips?
Share them with the flirting impaired at
www.marriable.com.

Planning Your Masterpiece

While some artists might claim last-minute inspiration ("It just came to me!"), most would swear by practice and planning. They focus on picking the right canvas, oil paints, watercolors, charcoal, or ink. Even the subject of the piece is decided before a brush is dipped in color.

The same goes for your first date. Nothing is worse for a woman than going out with a man who has nothing planned. "What do you wanna do?" "I don't care. What do you wanna do?" is not a good opening conversation. You don't have to have a minute-by-minute schedule of events, but you need a general idea of what's going to happen so that she doesn't have to do the heavy lifting. And girls, if you find yourself doing all the planning or making all the decisions, be prepared to make all the decisions for the rest of the relationship if you continue to go out with Mr. Lazy Wimpy Man.

To avoid being called Mr. LWM, you should have a plan before your date so you're not asking her to "go do something with you someday." Have a specific plan in mind when you ask her: "Hey, would you like to go to the park this weekend? They are doing Shakespeare in the Park on Saturday, and I hear it's pretty good." When you ask her out for a specific thing, you take the responsibility for what you will do together on your date firmly out of her hands and free her up to spend her time daydreaming about how much fun you'll have and poring over all her outfits to find the perfect thing for Shakespeare in the Park.

Exceptions to the plan: Of course, once you have a plan, you'll have to be ready and willing to alter it. Don't be so hardheaded and unwilling to go with the flow that you lose your date. If you wanted to go to a ball game but she has a headache and the crowd noise would kill her, be ready and willing to move on to something else.

Preplanning: Most women love the feeling of being pampered and cared for, and nothing screams care more than a man who has things taken care of. So if you are going to the opening night of a new movie, get the tickets in advance so it won't be sold out before you get there. You can even log on to movie websites and print your tickets from home if you can't get to the box office. Or if you are trying out a new restaurant, call and make reservations a few days

83

before. The thing that makes a woman melt is when a man is subtly in control. This isn't a loud, bossy kind of control; this is a man in control of his surroundings.

Plan a Date of Possible Progression

One of the most important things to remember when proposing a first date is leaving wiggle room to continue the date if it's going well but also having good points to stop early if you're just not feeling it. This is true for all first date scenarios, but especially when you barely know the person. We call this a date of possible progression.

For our first date, we met for coffee at Starbucks. After a little witty conversation and feeling a lot of chemistry (or was it the caffeine?), we decided to go for some chips and salsa at a local Mexican restaurant. While both of us had the option of bailing out after chips, we took the date even farther and stayed to order dinner. All of this from an innocent coffee date.

Women need to make sure they're not agreeing to a first date that doesn't give them a few escape hatches. Unless you *really* know the guy, only agree to a date that starts slow and seems short. You've got to be discriminating.

One word of warning to the guys out there: don't reveal your whole plan of progression to your date. When you've been having a great time over coffee and she hasn't hinted she's got somewhere else to be, then suggest your next destination for the date. ***Don't reveal the next two to eight steps!*** In other words, don't look desperate, but instead play it cool. Show that you're discriminating as well.

The Nuclear Option

In the dating world, sometimes you're going to get stuck on a date with someone you know in your very core is not the one for you. Worse yet, maybe your date isn't tracking with your faith, is getting all gropey, or is being constantly disrespectful. Hopefully you're on a date of progression, but if you've already committed to a longer date and your safety, dignity, or valuable free time needs to be rescued, invoke the nuclear option. End the date early or in midstream. Yes, it's awkward, but the rest of the night would be too. Wouldn't you at least like to salvage that?

The only reason you might think about enduring the misery (as long as you feel safe) is if you work with the person or see them all the time (i.e., at church). Under those circumstances, you don't want to seem cold and heartless unless they're completely unbearable. But if you are rarely or never going to see them again, push the button. Here's a short list of reasons to hit the big red button:

- Your date reveals they're married
- Your date reveals they're separated (still means married!)
- You told them to stop touching you and they keep invading your space
- They laugh at your most deeply held convictions or beliefs
- They're not really the gender you thought they were
- They're a blind date or "online find" and they grossly lied about their age or appearance (and it deeply bothers you)
- They won't let you go to an up or down vote

The easiest end-all statement is "I'm sorry, I'm going to have to end the date early. I wish you the best of luck in your search." Then stand up. Muscle memory makes them stand and expect you to leave. Don't fall into the trap of answering their "why?" questions. Just state that you can't see it working out, say I'm sorry again, and then move to the door.

A Planner Isn't a Dictator

Plans can be changed, as we've stated before. Be flexible. The best approach is to tell her what you have planned and then ask her how that sounds. If she frowns or squirms or just says yuck, don't get upset. Have a plan B. But if she is forever whining about what you are doing, don't get discouraged; consider it insight into this girl's mind. She might not be the one for you. After all, who wants to be with a complainer? She needs to be gracious enough to go with you on your plans most of the time. Look at this as a good test of her character. Does she go with the flow or try to manipulate and control everything in her world? That's the beauty of being a man early on. An important part of dating is finding out if this person is the one you want to spend the rest of your life with. And if you want to spend the rest of your life as a man, then you probably want to find a woman who is comfortable with that.

Guys on a Date: How to Be a Great First Date

Where to go. Remember, a date is a time for you two to talk. Girls love that! So don't take her to a movie or silent auction. Take her someplace where you two can talk and get to know each other.

Info. Let her know ahead of time how she should dress so she won't be in high heels and a dress for your hike around the lake.

Plan the date. Women love it when it looks like you've spent time planning something for them. Make plans. They don't have to cost you anything. Just have a plan of some kind.

Be on time. If you have to leave mega-early, then do it. Consider scoping out the best routes ahead of time so you don't get lost. Just don't get to her house late.

Door man. Get all doors for her. The car door, the restaurant door, get them all and let her go through first, unless it's a revolving door, in which case you go through first.

It's all about her. Ask her what kind of music she likes and play that. Don't have your favorite garage punk band or polka music blasting when you start the car.

Chair man. Pull out her chair for her and slowly push it in as she sits down. Then you can sit down.

Standing man. Stand up whenever she gets up from the table, enters the room, or leaves the room.

Ask her questions. Girls bond by talking. The more they can talk to you, the more they will like you. So make conversation. Talk with them, not at them.

Coat man. When she is putting on her coat, lift it up by the back of it and help her get into it.

No excuses. You really need to talk with your date.

Seating. If you do go to the movies, theater, church, or any other venue with row seating, let the girl walk into the row of seats before you.

Pay. If you asked her (which you'd better have), then you pay. No splitting *any* check.

Anticipation. At the end of a date, don't ask for another one. Save that for next time you talk.

Ideas for Date Conversation

Conversation is 50 percent of the grade on a first date. If a woman connects with a guy on a verbal/mental level, the guy would have to have major red flags in other areas to not get a second date. Here are some surefire ways of keeping the conversation rolling in your favor:

Ask her lots of questions about herself. Make them how, why, and when questions so she has to say more than yes and no back to you.

> » Where did you grow up?
> » How many brothers and sisters do you have?
> » Do you have any pets? What are their names?
> » What is one thing about you I might be surprised by?
> » What you do on weekends?
> » What are your favorite TV shows, sports teams, etc.?

Talk about your favorite hobby and why you like it. Then be sure to ask her what she thinks and what her fave hobby is.

Compliment something about her, then ask her a question about it.

> "I love your hair. Do you get a lot of compliments on it?"

> "I love your jeans. Where did you get them?"

Find out about her spirit. Ask her questions about her faith and her religious background.

Talk about the food. If you are eating together, always ask her how she likes the food. Find out what she likes best about it. Ask her about her favorite food in the world. If she could only eat one thing for the rest of her life, what would it be?

Ask her about her future. Talk about what you want to do, and find out what she dreams of.

Give-and-take is the key. Ask her questions, listen, talk a little about the same subject, then ask more questions. Keep the conversation going like a friendly game of volleyball, back and forth over the net.

I love your nose. Is it original? Not recommended unless dating in So. California.

Unveiling Your Masterpiece

Big Date Ideas

Here are some different date ideas that will help you make a great first impression.

Photo Shoot—Buy two disposable cameras and go somewhere like a train yard, flower farm, zoo, or any funky place around town and shoot 24 pics. Make them into an art project. Then plan a time to get back together and look over your pics. (Note: You take both cameras and develop them both. If you don't want a second date, then leave her with her own camera and let her develop the pics herself.)

If this is your talent, don't share.

Explore—Go somewhere neither of you has gone before.

Teach—Teach your date something that you do really well.

Taste Testing—Pick one kind of food or drink that she loves, like hot chocolate or apple pie, then go to four restaurants and judge each one based on the quality and taste. Talk about the food, the special tastes, the way it's served, the service. Make a night of being a food critic.

Q and A—Get a book of questions and spend the evening over dinner asking each other weird (but G-rated) stuff that you never would have thought of.

Theme Date—Find out what your date likes and build the date around that. If she loves Italy, make it an Italian night. Bring her Italian chocolate, take her to an Italian restaurant, buy an Italian CD to play in the car, and give her the CD when the night is over.

Vacation at Home—Never been a tourist in your own town? Well, give it a try. Go to the local visitors' bureau and scan the racks for touristy things to do in your area. The staff there can help you come up with all kinds of fun things to do. You can even decide to take a camera around with you and ask people to take pictures of you guys. Girls love memory-makers like photos.

Backwards dinner—Have dinner backwards, starting with dessert and working your way back.

Other Not-So-Different Date Ideas

Amusement parks

Bowling

Rollerblading

Hiking

Lunch in the park

Museum or art gallery

Visit an old folks home

Dance class

Pottery painting

Rock-climbing gym

Canoeing or boating

Play horseshoes

Walk on the beach

Golfing

Bike tour

How to Be the Perfect Guy: The Short List

First off, let's just get this out of the way. **Nobody** is perfect. But there are ways that guys can make women feel they're picking from the cream of the crop. Keep the following principles in mind when examining whether you're prime first date material not to mention **Marriable.**

Be Confident

Most guys confuse cockiness with confidence. But a cocky guy cares about himself and nobody else. A confident guy doesn't need attention but appreciates it when it's given and knows it might even be deserved! That's what separates a confident guy from just a caring guy. A caring guy looks after others, but doesn't necessarily think too much of himself. A confident guy not only looks after others, but he knows what he's got going for him.

Here's how a confident guy separates himself from the rest of the pack: by caring about other people, and not just his date. So talk to people, smile at them, and realize how valuable they all are. When you care for people, girls realize that you are a good guy. When a guy is really nice to a waiter—gets to know his name and talks with him more

95

like a person than a servant—something inside the girl goes "ding!" and she adds another point to your love bank. She thinks, "This isn't just an act with me, he treats everyone this way." You get good points for caring for people who can't do anything to get you what you want in life. So care about people; that's what makes you look confident. How do you do that? Here are some quick tips:

Talk to people in line with you. Make polite and witty conversation.

Tip people who are in the service industry. If you're too poor to tip, you're too poor to date. You should have enough in your date budget to give a guy a few bucks for helping you out with something.

Help other women get doors and carry things. When you care about all people, she digs it. But remember, your date is always first on your list. Don't run off to help someone and leave her hanging.

No, no, I'll get the door for you too.

Unveiling Your Masterpiece

Don't yell at people when you drive. Rage is bad.

Don't be afraid to talk to anyone—old people, young people, talk to them all.

Communicate

Now, we're definitely not asking you to get all girly and get in touch with your feminine side, heaven forbid. We want you to be a guy through and through, but we also want you to understand how you can meet the needs of the girl you are dating. We want you to be prepared to treat her the way she was made to be treated, and that means you have to learn a little bit about communication. It's the biggest, most important thing for women. They live for it. They love it. They are all about the talking. The fact of the matter is, they are never really going to totally shut up, and you don't want them to, because when they talk, they fall in love. No talky, no lovey. So what's the deal with communicating with girls? How can you do it so you are still a guy but also a girl magnet? Here are a few things you need to know about how girls operate. Try some of them out and see if they don't work for you.

After your date, call her. It's normal in girl world to call each other after doing something just to talk about it and confirm that it was really great. So if it was your first date, call her two to three days after the date. Tell her how great it was. Talk about some of the stuff you did and why you liked it. This would also be a good time to ask her out again.

Tell her what you like about her so far. You probably barely know this woman, so don't pour it on too strong. Be genuine and talk about what she's got going for her.

Ask her questions. The key to communicating with a girl is letting her talk. And the best way for her to talk is to talk about good things. Don't let her get caught up in telling you all her miseries; rehearsing all the crap in her life only makes her more depressed. Ask her stuff like, "If you could live anywhere in the world, where would it be?" or "If money were no object and you could do whatever you want for the rest of your life, what would it be?" Find a book of questions and pull it out for an occasional chat session.

Give her a little gift, like some little trinket for her desk or nightstand. Make sure it matches her style and taste, and don't spend much on it. You don't want to feel bitter if things don't work out. Look at the gift as a throwaway. Don't make a big production of giving it to her (don't wrap it), but pull it out of your pocket as an afterthought and move the conversation on after she thanks you. A gift communicates that you like her and were thinking about her when you saw it.

Compliment her. Remember, compliments communicate a lot to a girl. Be sure to notice how nice her hair is, her nails, her clothes, and so on.

Look her in the eye when she talks. When she is telling you something, don't look around the room. Don't watch TV or get distracted by stuff going on around you. To girls, it means you aren't listening if you aren't looking them in the eyes. So keep your eyes on her.

Stop clowning around and look her in the eyes, bozo.

Sympathize with her. When she is bummed or angry about something, don't try to correct her and fix the problem. Just tell her how bad you feel for her and let her vent on you. The best thing you can do

99

for a girl is sympathize with her feelings, not try to change them.

Bring her flowers. The whole thing of a gift is often overlooked by guys, but as we said before, gifts don't have to be expensive to score major points with girls. If you don't have much cash, stop by a vacant field and pick wildflowers. Wrap them in newspaper and a bow. She'll love the effort. Oh, and roses? Those are kind of serious, so save those for the proposal. Get creative. Find other kinds of flowers like tulips or daisies, ones that are unique and fit her personality.

Girls on a Date: How to Be a Great First Date

The thing to remember while on a date with a guy is that, ahem, well, uh, *he is the guy*. Seems obvious, we know, but it really isn't as easy as it sounds. On a date your job is not to be in charge; it is not to control the conversation, the stuff you do, or the time it takes to do it. Remember, you aren't out with your best girlfriend, so it isn't a crab session or a tell-me-your-life-history event. It's a chance for him to see if you are chaseable and for you to see if you want to be chased.

Taboo Topics for the Date

Don't talk about . . .

    your ex-boyfriend(s)

    your family or roommate problems

    your pet's incontinence

    anything negative

    your health problems

    how much you want to get married

    how much you like him

Surefire Ways to Keep His Fire Going

The fact that he asked you out is a good sign, but you want to keep him wanting you. Here are 13 surefire ways to keep his fire going:

1. Don't offer to meet him somewhere. Let him come get you. He loves that part.
2. Slow down and let him get doors. That's him showing you that he is a gentleman, so don't try to steal that job from him. (Note: if it's a revolving door, let him go in first so he can push it.)

3. Don't reach across the car and unlock his door. If you were considered important enough to have your door opened, you shouldn't then have to reach across, especially if you are nicely dressed, and unlock his side. Some guys might think this is unkind of you, but when you *do* reach across they know deep down that their service to you of opening your door isn't as special. Remote door locks are making this one obsolete anyway.

4. At the movies or theater, once you both agree on the best place to sit, go into the row of seats first.

5. Talk about good things. Don't whine about your trials and tribulations.

6. Laugh at his jokes (or his attempts at jokes).

7. If he is talking too much, don't ask him a lot of questions. He doesn't bond by talking like you do, so if you think that asking him questions makes him like you more, you are wrong. It just makes him like *him* more. Let him ask *you* questions, and if he doesn't, then feel free to just interrupt him to make comments on what he is saying. Guys interrupt each other; that's how they talk. They don't ask questions. So feel free to be part of the conversation and cut in. Don't change the subject; just join in.

8. Let him pay, and then say, "Thank you for dinner. That was so nice of you. I loved it." (Note: Once you go out with a guy a lot, you can start to offer to pay every so often. But not all the time, and definitely not on the first date.) This is a big part of letting him lead. It is a symbol that he is a provider and protector.

9. Let him plan the date. Some guys have no idea how to do this, but they should. If he asks, he plans. If he doesn't plan, then you can make a suggestion, but don't take that role away from him. If he wants to date you, he should be man enough to plan.

10. Let him get your chair. A true gentleman will pull out your chair for you and slowly push it in as you sit down. Smile and say thank you.

11. Eat. Order a sensible meal, meaning one you can eat. And then eat it. Don't order a steak and then not touch it—oooh, he hates that—or a small salad and water. You eat, so don't pretend you don't. Guys love to see a girl with a good appetite. It's one of the things they find attractive in girls, and they don't worry about you having an eating disorder.

12. Make conversation, but if he is really nervous and talks about himself the entire time, don't get upset. That's just his way of telling you how much of a catch

103

he is and how much he wants to prove to you that he's worthy of you. By the second date he should be more calm and open to hearing from you.

13. Don't call him the next day or even the next week. Let him call you. You are the one who is being chased, not the chaser. Call him first and we guarantee you'll move 5 points from the hotness scale over to the desperate scale.

Talking on the Phone with Guys

There are several phases involved in talking on the phone with the male species. Only phase one pertains to the first date realm, but we'll include the other two as a bonus.

Phase 1—In the beginning of the relationship, you want to let the guy chase you. So it goes like this: if he is just starting to show an interest in you, the last thing he needs is a marathon conversation. We know, for you it's a bonding moment, but for him it's too long for a conversation to go. So if you want to really get him to like you and want to call you back again, keep it short. Talk 15–20 minutes max. If he is still talking after that long, tell him you really have to go, but you really enjoyed talking to him. This way when he gets off the phone he isn't saying, "Sheesh, that girl can talk." He's saying, "Wow, I really like her. I can't wait to talk to her again." So try to keep it short in the beginning of the relationship.

Phase 2—This is when you've been on a few dates. You are starting to feel more comfortable with each other, and he's starting to call more often. This is when you get to find out a lot about each other and start to become some sort of item. We still recommend keeping the convos short, but you can ramp them up to 30 minutes or an hour. But don't go over that, or you run the risk of giving too much info. Remember, guys are hunters; they like the hunt and the chase. Don't be like the deer who just walks out and goes, "Here I am! Shoot me!" That's no fun at all. Don't hang on the phone too long, and he'll be dying to call you back.

Phase 3—In phase three you are an item. You've been going out for quite a while, and you spend a lot of time together. You might even say you're best friends. If he is really wanting to talk and still calling you a lot, then you can ramp up your chats based on how much you think he is enjoying them. If you are the only one talking most of the time, then he is probably not having the best time of his life, so take it easy on the guy. Spend some of that talking energy on your girlfriends. They were made for it. He wasn't.

Guys Not to Date

- Don't date guys with different religious beliefs than you
- Don't date a guy who has a rep of being a user
- Don't date your best friend's ex
- Don't date someone just because you were afraid to say no when he asked you out
- Don't date a guy who makes you feel ugly
- Don't date a guy who cuts you down, even if he says he's sorry
- Don't date a guy who tries to control you with words or violence
- Don't date a guy because you feel sorry for him
- Don't date a guy more than once when there's no chemistry

The ~~Art~~ Curse of
the Nice Guy

7

While we go into more detail on why "Nice Guys Really Do Finish Last" in *Marriable*, it's an important topic that we should cover here to explain why nice guys are typically at a disadvantage during the ask and the first date compared to the bad boy.

The Initial Attraction of the Bad Boy

The "bad boy" that girls squirm over typically seems to have a well-defined personality. He has a style all his own. He has a suave confidence that might almost look like arrogance to some, but at least he knows who he is and what he wants. He's a man's man. Firm, confident, nearly silent, with a wry smile. He doesn't smile a lot like a schoolgirl. He doesn't get overly excited or giddy. Remember when Tom Cruise was jumping up and down on Oprah's couch? He suddenly lost his edge (and his mind).

He doesn't have a bunch of girlfriends who consider him just one of the girls. He has the typically male characteristics that draw the attention of the female. When he picks her up for a date, he isn't standing at attention like a love-struck schoolboy; he is calm and casual, in control. If he offers flowers, they look almost like an afterthought, not a bouquet he spent hours searching for. His understated actions make the female think perhaps he's had so much experience dating that it isn't anything new . . . and that must mean a lot of girls like him . . . and therefore he must be quite a catch. Follow the female logic?

Girls yearn for the bad boy because he seems to know more than he's letting on. He doesn't gush over her. He clearly likes her, but he's holding something back, and that's intriguing. He isn't afraid to ask her out or to take her hand or to lead the way. In her estimation he is a real man, and what's most important is that he makes her feel like a real woman. Why? Because he has no female characteristics that compete with her own. Instead, he seems to need her to bring the female traits to the relationship. It's a perfect union, each filling in where the other is lacking. And for all intents and purposes, nothing we've described here is **bad.** In essence, we've described the "great guy"—except that the bad boy often uses his manly wiles to play his unguarded female victims.

The Nice Guy on a Date

Now let's have a look at the "nice guy." This is the guy who is all about the girl. He listens intently, he responds appropriately, he talks of his heart and his feelings just as he's been told that girls like. He is transparent and giving of his emotions and his thoughts. He wants to create a bond with the girl that is similar to one she might have with her best friend. He caters to her every need; he even anticipates them.

These things aren't bad in and of themselves, but when it begins to appear that he lives for the attention of the female, she starts to wonder. "So early in the relationship and he already seems to think I hung the moon. He obviously doesn't know me," she thinks to herself. "Am I his last and only option?" His premature and inaccurate evaluation of her perfection leaves her suspicious.

And when he makes it very clear early on that he adores her, even loves her, the jig is up. The girl can no longer handle the overly emotional and emotive male who seems to be responding like she longs to respond in a healthy relationship. Essentially he takes her role on himself and rides it like a weary horse. This leaves the girl feeling anything but feminine.

The Great Guy?

Now this might irritate some of you, but we tend to shy away from defining the Great Guy or Dream Woman simply because it creates a checklist of "Mr./Ms. Perfect." A great guy tends to be a mix of the nice guy and bad boy. A guy who's capable of caring for others and putting himself last but at the same time can be confident, self-assured, and in control of his surroundings. In other words, it depends a lot on the situation and the person.

See? None of that is easily broken down into a top ten list of qualities to look for. It more has to do with balance and personal preference. Seems lame, we know, but we're not looking to build a race of man-bots here, just trying to help the nice guys find some balance. The bad boys know they need reforming, that's why they're called **bad.** Nice guys aren't too far away from being great, they just need to learn why bad boys seem manlier to women than the nice guys.

111

Not Nice, Not Bad, but Great

In review, nice guys are desperate to share too much too soon, while bad boys are desperate to bury their softer side as a flawed weakness. Meanwhile, back on the estrogen ranch, girls who date bad boys are desperate to believe they can change them, and girls who date nice guys are soon freaked out when the niceys share too much too soon. Finding the chewy middle in between will help the nice guy become a truly great date.

The Art of Saying
Goodnight

8

If your date didn't go so well, or if you have a problem with rejecting people or handling it yourself, consider picking up our book *The Art of Rejection*. It goes into far more detail on helping people who can't say no or are afraid of hearing no, especially when it comes to dating. But for now, let's assume your first date went smashingly because of the advice you took from *Marriable* and *The Art of the First Date*. So how do you part ways for the night gracefully?

The key in saying goodnight or ending your date is the age-old entertainment adage: "Always leave them wanting more." Your date should be anticipating your next date (or hoping there'll be a next date) when you say goodnight, not feeling so exhausted or spent that all they can think about is their pillow or how soon their morning is coming.

If you knew your date beforehand (close family friend, longtime co-worker, etc.) and you decided to share transportation (still not recommended on the first date), the man should always walk the woman to her door. The man

114

should also "stop short"—say, one step lower than the door itself—to say goodnight, leaving a safety halo around the woman so she knows he's not going in for the goodnight kiss.

Never, ever go for a kiss on the first date. It screams "I do this all the time." Also, don't participate in the easily confused "just friends hug" or "pity hug." Using a hug to replace a goodnight kiss is just plain lame and can give off way too many mixed signals. If he had a good time, he'll call for a second date. If she had a good time, she'll say yes.

No pity hugs please.

Guys, if you had a great time and want to go out again, listen for clues in her good-bye, like "We'll have to go back to that restaurant and try that dessert." Don't blurt out, "HOW ABOUT TOMORROW?" Show some cool and say, "Definitely. I'll give you a call this week and we'll set it up." She'll love that you're not desperate, and it'll also give you time to plan more than just dessert.

There's a classic episode of **Seinfeld** where George adopts a new philosophy in all social situations: ***always leave them wanting more***.

The Art of Saying Goodnight

The same is imperative for the first date. If you wear out your welcome by trying to extend the date past the other person's energy level or overall interest, you've just created a bad ending to an otherwise successful evening. When looking to end the date, just repeat to yourself, "Always leave them wanting more." You might even tuck away another golden oldie, "All's well that ends well."

Soooo . . . how'd it go?!

Share your first date triumphs
with us at www.marriable.com.

Remember, there's not one mathematical way to paint a landscape or sculpt a statue. Embrace dating as an art and rediscover your masculinity or femininity in the process. Throw off your lab coat, drop your beaker, and grab a brush. Put your thumb up and start painting!

Hayley DiMarco writes cutting-edge and bestselling books including *Mean Girls*, *Mean Girls All Grown Up*, *Sexy Girls*, *Technical Virgin*, *Marriable*, and *Dateable*. Her goal is to give practical answers for life's problems and to encourage readers to form stronger spiritual lives. Hayley is Chief Creative Officer and founder of Hungry Planet, an independent publishing imprint and communications company that feeds the world's appetite for truth. Hungry Planet helps organizations understand and reach the multitasking mind-set, while Hungry Planet books tackle life's everyday issues with a distinctly modern spiritual voice.

Michael DiMarco has worked in publisher relations, coached volleyball at the university level, and co-hosted a relationship humor radio show called *Babble of the Sexes*. He is the CEO and Publisher of Hungry Planet, working with authors who wish to reach an increasingly postmodern culture with premodern truth. Michael is the coauthor of *Marriable*, *The Art of the First Date*, and *The Art of Rejection* with his wife, Hayley, and they live in Nashville, Tennessee.

"Feeding the World's Appetite for Truth"

What makes Hungry Planet books different?

Every Hungry Planet book attacks the senses of the reader with a post-modern mind-set (both visually and mentally) in a way unlike most books in the marketplace. Attention to every detail from physical appearance (book size, titling, cover, and interior design) to message (content and author's voice) helps Hungry Planet books connect with the more "visual" reader in ways that ordinary books can't.

With writing and packaging content for the young adult and "hip adult" markets, Hungry Planet books combine cutting-edge design with felt-need topics, all the while injecting a much-needed spiritual voice.

Why are publishers so eager to work with Hungry Planet?

Because of the innovative success and profitable track record of HP projects from the best-selling *Dateable* and *Mean Girls* to the Gold Medallion-nominated *The Dirt on Sex* (part of HP's The Dirt series). Publishers also take notice of HP founder Hayley (Morgan) DiMarco's past success in creating big ideas like the "Biblezine" concept while she was brand manager for Thomas Nelson Publishers' teen book division.

How does Hungry Planet come up with such big ideas?

Hayley and HP general manager/husband Michael DiMarco tend to create their best ideas at mealtime, which in the DiMarco household is around five times a day. Once the big idea and scope of the topic are established, the couple decides either to write the content themselves or find an up-and-coming author with a passion for the topic. HP then partners with a publisher to create the book.

How do I find out more about Hungry Planet?

Use the Web, silly—www.hungryplanet.net

Still waiting?

Take the desperate out of dating!

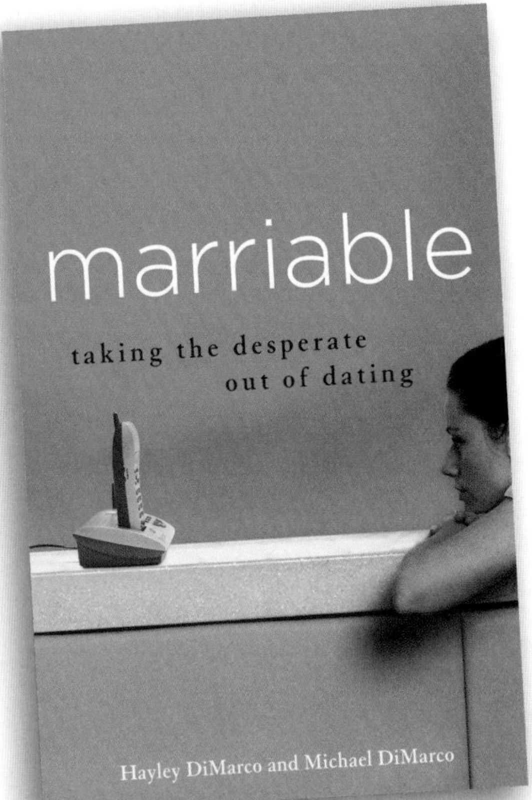

Join Hayley and Michael as they help you expose and eliminate your desperate dating habits.

Available at your local bookstore

Revell
www.revellbooks.com

Hungry Planet
www.hungryplanet.net